~~w you!
Best idea ever!
creative
lioness!
♡ Ashley

With a Hunger
I Didn't Know
I Had

With a Hunger I Didn't Know I Had
ISBN: 978-0-9937911-2-3

First edition

Cover and interior design: encreLibre
Published by encreLibre 2016
encreLibre.com

For Alex

Acknowledgments

Thank you to Alex Archibald, who photo-graphed the front cover. I'd also like to give thanks to the other people who inspired these poems, and to Salt Spring Island, for holding me, rocking me, and eventually pushing me out, during the year that I wrote this book. I am grateful to my friends and family for all their support, and to anyone who takes the time to read poetry in an age where it isn't so popular. This book is about hunger, and about longing: an ancient expression of the human soul, a cave; I hope you find yourself in there. And I hope you find some comfort in seeing the scratches on the walls: the evidence that this is a story that at least one other person has lived through. Thank you for your support.

But Oh, How Delicious It Would Be....

Meeting Ganesh Again

For days I knelt
at the foot of Ganesh,
prostrated and wept,
cursed new beginnings
and most of all,
the end.
I wanted to know how he did it:
danced into unfamiliar lands,
his fat toes light as the petals
that adorned his neck.
I wanted to know
how he so joyfully transitioned,
how he embraced change,
and most of all,
how he let go.
I wondered if
he ever sobbed
at the sight of his elephant head
in the mirror,
if he ever missed his human skin–
if his trunk felt awkward,
his ears too large and hollow.
I wanted to know if he
understood me:
god of new directions never before
dreamed of,
or necessarily desired–
or if I had to rely on Tara
for that kind of compassion.
Sweet elephant child,
please,
just tell me you understand–
that you've lost everything too,
and started fresh,
and that, at least at first,
it wasn't always so easy for you.

Gwendolyn

She's always by the sea
at night, raking moonbeams
into her wheelbarrow, trying to capture
the beauty: a museum
for planets and fog.
And she crawls
in tall grass,
like a spider, picking silk with bony
fingers,
wrapping gossamer around her heart
torn apart in eight places, the sting
of the love that left her.
Do not go near, or look
her in the eye;
she is bound
to bewitch you, or send
you reeling with your own disease–
the contagiousness of madness, and how
the only vaccines around only treat
the symptoms.
There was a time
when she was the most beautiful girl
you'd ever seen, the whole of her
wrapped
in magic and stardust.
But now
she is gaunt, and vacant, and chasing
illusions
upon still and shining waters,
as if they were silver leaves
fallen, like Eve,
from trees made
of all of the things
the moon dreams about.

1929

All I really want to do
on this early Sunday winter morning
is play
the trumpet with a band
in a small living room, with
a giant window, with
white light bathing the walls and
hardwood floor–
even though I don't play the trumpet,
let alone have a band, or know any
old timey songs.
It would be wonderful;
it would be lovely:
to spend my days,
carefully; choosing which wooden chair
upon which to sit, which
dusty rose house dress to wear, and how
to cut my hair
to my chin, with curls,
the way the girls
from the 1920's did–
even though I was born in the 80's,
and have little knowledge of what it means
to do the Charleston
with the neighbours, or wear
a string of pearls
convincingly.
But oh,
how delicious it would be
to relish an afternoon in a small house
on a quiet street, playing folk music with a group
of passionate people,
who died long before we turned into machines.

Wreck of a Ship

You don't slam doors anymore–
don't smash pans onto stove-tops,
or gulp leftover
boxed Pinot Gris
from potted mugs:
don't apologize between hugs
with "I love you"s and "I'm sorry"s, then
sink quietly
into a hot bath of bubbles
up to your ears, and
blast Tom Waits records
from the living room wall-unit,
sinking deeper
until the house disappears,
and Alice is but a dream–
someone you loved long ago
who will never return
from her spot in the ice; her fishing hole,
or break your heart again.
You wish for those days now,
from that single bed at your sister's,
getting what you wanted–
her crooked wand, erasing,
a silhouette of crows, murdering.
And Alice is but a memory,
a name you lost yourself in,
a flame that burned you and then went out;
there is nothing to warm you now but your wounds.
Things burn up easily these days,
or else fade:
like old love letters, promises, and ships–
even ice melts, leaving you asleep
in a thawed out pond, ten days removed
from Alice, her name
no longer written there–with skates
still on your feet.

Chalk

You've been erased, somehow,
chalk on a blackboard,
wiped clean by the custodian
on a Friday night
after everyone has gone home.
Empty hallways buzz with silence;
not even ghosts live here.
Your face is a blur,
your voice
melts with his–
the first one to ever occupy
this corner of my heart;
is there room for you now?
You pervade it,
both of you,
perfume, inhaling,
chalk dust, choking,
gasoline, asphyxiating,
making fires bigger and brighter.
My memory of you burns away–
smoking cigarettes in the schoolyard;
all of our memories dissipating,
the teacher's screams carried away,
swallowed,
by some gust of wind,
with ashes blazing.
Am I not even granted the realness of
how it felt to love you?
Now, in my dreams,
you are the same person:
his body and your heart–
a mask with distorted features,
as if standing before a broken mirror,
the one that almost smashed on my head
six years ago when I lived at the ocean's edge–
the spell will be broken soon
I'm certain.
I wonder why it is
that even photographs won't resurrect you,

why it is that I seem to forget so fast,
sand slipping through silken fingers,
water,
tears,
the seconds that tick-tock
and disappear–
where will our memories rush to
once we've finally
let go?
When will we leave that school,
the place for so many lessons–
where we destroyed our illusions,
took off our masks,
put down the chalk–
and walk home?

Dirty Laundry

You were a clean sheet when I met you:
barely twenty and still a gentleman:
properly raised, the kind
who respects
women and doesn't forget to say
thank you–
you could've kissed me last night–
hell–
you could have done anything–
the point is that you didn't.
The point is that you wouldn't.
You're in love with a girl as idealistic as you,
away at university, studying to become a nurse–
you lit up when I asked you to describe her,
your first love, and as far as you're concerned,
your only.
And I do not envy
the heartbreak that will inevitably come
when she calls you, sobbing,
telling you she's lied, telling you
she's met someone–
when you find
out that there are so many interesting men
in the city:
men with wit and fire–
men who know how to seduce and suggest,
men with cars and cigarettes, and
black irises and magic, and wicked,
wicked words
with whom she loves
to philosophize and debate,
and she
has been lonely and forgetful,
and wrapped up in her new life,
and so incredibly excited.
So you keep the fire burning
in her absence, abstaining from
women ten years older than you,
damaged, with scars

on their chests, who
lean in near and whisper drunken confessions
on Tuesday nights
and hold you close on carpeted floors, feeling,
even in their inebriation, your discomfort:
"I have a girlfriend."
Did I kiss your neck? I swear I must have kissed
    your neck.
And you remind me
of a younger, sweeter
part of myself,
lost
in the laundry basket:
piles of heartbreak over more heartbreak–the
    men
I held onto and had to tear myself away from,
when I believed
in happy endings.
When I believed
that my body was worth saving–
when I believed
that there was something sacred about
uttering the word "love."
And you are beautiful, and wholesome, and
    good,
and I want
you to stay this way.
If you can, just please
stay this way–
and marry her, and make babies, and grow old
    together,
and tell me
that during that year when she was away
she went back to her room alone every night
and dreamed only of you.
Tell me the college boys had nothing on you,
that she kept all your letters and secrets,
your hurt and terrified places,
that she kept her promises and integrity
and your heart
safe
from breaking.

I so badly want to believe it's still possible
that a love so pure,
so tender,
and so bright
exists
somewhere in this mess.
If you can keep it together, it is almost as if
there is a chance I might
find it again.

From Casket To Cradle

Christ was a Woman

You were born
of a woman screaming
your mother
crying out
blood and other fluids
a small sexual hole now a
gaping void
a cave
with scratches on the inside
squeezing your head
her tears and swearing
your father the culprit
for doing this to her
she's certain
give me the drugs
she shouts
wanting so badly to ease it
you were born of her suffering
But that isn't enough
no
go back further
your father suffered too
masturbating
under sheets in the dark
fifteen years old and porno magazines
trying to cool the fever
the loneliness
of what it means to be born alone
a lifeboat
separate from god
when he met your mother he couldn't believe it
finally
a woman to love him
someone
to make him feel less lonely
and your mother's eggs
dropping
month after month
through her cervix

a tunnel of death
monthly bloodletting
a ritual for witches
counting down the years
until she is barren
unable to attract or give life
the one thing she's sure she's good for
why must women give birth
in order to feel that they've contributed
        something
a brand new life
reincarnated
from casket to cradle
a new angel to care for you
we hope to have girls
or sensitive boys
because the world needs saving
but there are too many wailing Marys in
        Jerusalem
and crucifixion is not a fate a mother wishes
upon her child

While he Lights the Fire

Cold October sun sinks seamlessly behind
rosy gold on the deep lake, still,
except for the ripples, breath of clouds,
      mother
smoothing bedtime blankets and night
      clothes,
six o'clock,
and you, in your grey sweater,
nose cold: all of those early mornings
when the fire went out.
You wish, in your secret place,
with Christmas lights,
for a new lover familiar as the sound of your
      heartbeat, someone
to hold you strong,
someone to light the wood stove again, and
boil the water
for your morning bath–
sponge the weariness from your shoulders
      and spine
like paint–
someone to create a world with.
And in your secret place, with
oranges and tea, you wish
for another human voice,
breath from another set of lips
on your collarbone and the space between
your shoulder blades, and what
it might mean
to run for shelter in the smell of his neck and
burrow deep in warm blankets with him:
pair of bright eyes twinkling
at your voice
giving sound to the new dawn.
Softly, he tells you to stay in bed.
He takes the dog out and makes the porridge.
And this, you understand,
is what will haunt you when it's over:
his careful disentanglement,

and his slippers dragging across hardwood
    floors,
squeak of handles turning,
and the slow crackling
of kindling: the weight
of his body sliding back down
next to yours,
arm around your torso:
and the coolness of his palm
on your mouth. And this,
you understand, is what
will break your heart when it's over:
kneeling before an empty fireplace,
striking matches in the dark.

Porous

I could tell he was still
in love with his ex–
it was written all over his pupils:
oyster shells bursting with black pearls:
secrets seeped out of his pores like sweat.
And it was okay,
it was more than okay,
though he was shy about what he oozed,
what he shouted,
though he said nothing–
his wounds, gashed open:
it's true I have a nose
for blood,
with sores of my own.
I told him I wasn't threatened,
and there was nothing to be embarrassed
          about;
he hugged me then,
exhaling.
I only wanted us to be ourselves.
Isn't that all a person can hope for?
After enough heartbreak I've grown
          accustomed
to the running of water and
the changing of moon shapes,
the inevitability of birth and death,
and to the fickle and forgetful
heart of the human.
And who am I to shut a door
for which I have no key?
And in this violent and unfeeling world
don't you think we need
more love
not less?
I let him go then:
a moving ship in a harbour opening
to the sea, waved goodbye,
and planted
his DNA in my tissues–

love for the goddess of many aspects:
creation in all its forms–
a seed.

Mad Girl in my Head

She's been locked in that basement for years, with
only meshes of afternoon light streaming in–
the dusty piano her only companion–
no one listens to her music, though,
or turns on the lights.
I suppose her eyes have grown accustomed to the
      dark now,
like those of bats and other nocturnal creatures.
She pleads, "Let me out,"
"Please, somebody let me out."
I want to set her free. This is no way to treat
      an animal
let alone a human being.
"Get the nurse," another woman says.
"It isn't safe here."
The next thing I know we're in the mental
      hospital,
the old fashioned kind, with all of those shades of
      white–
the nurse comes out and puts her
on a leash:
she bites and kicks, punches and screams.
She is uncontrollable.
And now I'm the one in the basement, alone this
      time.
I run my hands over the scratched piano.
I see the broken chains,
the stuffed bird
with a nail through its chest.
And it occurs to me that she has escaped.
Then the doorbell.
I know she's close, she's here, she's at the door–
I climb out the window.
I begin to run, but my feet are so heavy,
and she's right behind me.
This is when I realize I've been dreaming.
I charge at her, screaming like a wild animal,
but my hands shake, and I'm not strong enough–
and all that's left now is her,

sitting atop my bloody body,
stuffing her red mouth with my heart.
Mad girl in the basement:
what do you have to say?
What songs exist in your fingertips,
what songs want to be heard
on that old piano?
I can't let you out again,
but I can listen.
It's not fair to lock you up under the guise
of taking care of you,
it isn't enough to put you to sleep:
an artificial coma in which you can still dream,
with all of those ghosts tormenting you—
please, sick sister: tell me about it.
Tell me all of your nightmares:
all of those demons and voices.
I promise I won't run,
or let them hurt you again.

Violets

His music is a Cathedral stuffed
with violets–
petals and perfume protruding
from stained glass and wooden doors,
heavy with secrets and history:
the austerity of a thousand Wednesdays,
with ashes soiling your third eye,
a Puja for the lineage that came
before him:
Fahey and Jones, and all of those blind boys and girls
wailing on guitars in the early 20's,
marking the roots
of folk music in America.
Persephone has come again,
has graced groundhogs with her shadow,
sinewy and floral, a wreath
of life and roots
and bamboo shoots
through a blanket of snow, and crocuses unveiling
their faces, tender and vibrant,
shy and perfect and unapologetic, that shout,
"Here I am!"
in their vulnerability,
in their humility,
in their beauty that will not
shrink away from the ice and wind,
or hide from view, or wait
until the ground has properly thawed.
His music
is a garden of snowdrops crammed into
a church–choirs raising
the hairs on the back of your neck,
hymns of angels and a love
so pure and strong you can only scarcely
remember it: from a time
when you lived beneath tulips and daffodils,
and too many suns to tell time by.
His music is a locked door
to a confessional kicked open by a sinner,

an addict who refuses to believe
in a hell from which there is no exit,
in a God who won't believe in him,
in a hundred Hail Marys falling
on the deaf ears of a virgin.
It is a window
shattered by heavenly voices,
with the scent of earth and sex
breezing in, the way some of the nicest flowers
        still smell like semen.
His music
is the sound of my soul:
two guitars resonating in E Minor:
reverberating in similar frequencies,
crumbling Cathedral walls, with
doves flying north over fields of oleanders,
their sweat bleeding fragrance and music
into your ears:
His music
is a field of poppies.
I walk between silent crosses
remembering.
Even in the stillness
I can hear it.

Heart Advice for Difficult Times

What I want for you more than anything
is not to miss it:
the deer grazing in your snowy yard
by the icy lake at nightfall–
how you'll have to leave your room,
creak downstairs, the warmth of the fireplace:
a blanket warming you
in increments,
and stand on the coffee table
to get a good look–
how she'll go on, with her eyelashes,
wisps of silver,
her tail white as the three-quarter moon.
I want you to feel it: the cold coming in,
in stages, as the day draws to a close,
red and magenta oil pastels
on a white canopy, your breath
rising chimney smoke, the snow
crunching beneath your boots,
how you'll wish you would have worn a warmer coat,
your fingers freezing,
observing, as you might be blind
tomorrow–you soak it in–
winter trees scratching blue rainclouds, thick
with the tears of a compassionate god.
I want you to feel it: the void
that fills you–cry as if you'll never
come up for air, or leave this place.
Feel the loss of what you expected,
all of your plans and hopes, your big dreams,
and bury them now, on the ocean floor,
pearls and opals to be dug up by the next
children who come here, hoping for comfort,
hoping for some release, some balm,
for this world, this body of salt water
without a shoreline.
Feel your legs burning,
your heart pounding,
your lungs about to explode–

how much more can a person endure?
Embrace it like you would a newborn child,
as you would yourself.
This is your initiation into humanity.
And when the heartbreak has run its course,
pneumonia,
feel the fever break, your sweat cooling.
And watch the deer grazing by a snowy lake
before dark, and feel the relief
of a thousand waning moons,
the absence of tears, the beating of your heart
settling back into sinus, your lungs
free again.
And whatever you do, remember to breathe
love back into the world.
People have suffered long before
your little human birth,
and will continue.
Practice kindness.

Smoke Signals

Black Widow

This dervish dancing, toes
twirling, silk splicing
spirited spider
has gotten sick: my house
on fire, my web
ripped apart
by flaming corn brooms and sticks–
knitting needles spinning
yarn: splintered:
indigo and crimson–
circling; weaving;
dancing with Rumi in a cyclone at dawn.
And you are not who
you said you were: spinning
webs close to Earth:
in outer space, your home
unifying planets and stars.
Saturn slides south again,
a broken limb in a sling,
your toothy grin and
sooty linen soiled
from sunny afternoons spent
inhaling too much sage and
cedar, snaking into nostrils,
sending smoke signals to
cellar ceilings,
serenading mermaids and muses,
drunk off marmalade in the early evening,
        the sky
mandarin and magenta.
You are not who you said
you were–
spinning your web around me:
a straitjacket
handcuffing me to false
niceness and
unknowing compassion.
A spider liquidates your organs, and sucks
them through a straw.

I should have known you
were one when you said
it was your favourite animal.

Northern Life

Snow doesn't glitter here,
diamonds and sapphires,
ice castles and queens without hearts–
it is brown
slush and dirt
real as the hands of a working man,
sobering
the morning after
in bed with a bare-faced woman–
spring will not come any time soon.
And I write the poems
that want to be born
the poems that come to me,
in moments of remembering and forgetting
clarity and chaos,
order and oblivion–
my home chose me.
The North as I love it
hasn't changed,
except for that giant pink sign:
"You are beautiful"
in block letters
on the side of a brick building
downtown–
are we trying to be someone we are not?
A mother doesn't choose her child:
it chooses her–
do not be so silly as to think
I can just sit down and write
a love song,
a ballad about you–
all of the hurt you left me with,
and send it in to Nashville
for fame and a thousand dollars.
I sit alone in restaurants,
high on stools, writing–
I order a Tusker,
"do you guys still have that?"
I remember the taste:

water and wheat,
diluted,
I'm a woman who knows what she likes.

Beach Behaviour

I don't hate him,
she says:
I did–
but I don't anymore.
My parents never fought,
so I didn't know how to do it.
I just remember a gut feeling
that this was wrong.
And he would tell me,
"your feelings are wrong."
But how can you say that to someone?
You remember it differently.
"She's such a lovely woman."
Nothing negative–
or real–
to say about her.
I want to say that it's different
for a woman:
that all of the ways you've hurt her
are not so easily forgotten–
that she's had to work on
rebuilding her heart,
a castle made of blood,
into a forgiving place,
and there haven't been many others
to share her bed.
But you carry this divorce
around with you, too:
a bucket of pointy rocks–
and your lungs ache
with the breath of a thousand inhalations–
       you fear
what might happen if
you let the air out–
and the distractions
of attempts at starting over,
rebuilding sand castles,
when the tide is coming in,
and your heart has grown calluses

whose edges dig into your tissues.
You need to cry:
need to let out the years
and decades of brave and happy
faces–let them crumble, the way
castles always do
when the waves come.

Vine

I was writing in my journal
scheming–
how I was going to play this–
how I was going to outwit you.
The things lovers do when the love is gone,
and all that remains
is desire
and some longing to be held
in the place
where you last left me
wanting.
I thought of processing with you,
of telling you
how I felt,
what I was thinking, asking why
we couldn't just share
like we'd once shared,
down to the silences, stripped
the language
from clothes and skin–
I wanted to touch you.
I wanted to feel your heart inside of me.
Or maybe I just wanted to get into your pants,
the way a predator does.
And I'm not sorry for that.
For being aggressive.
But I also thought of ignoring you,
of calling another lover.
I did neither of these things.
Instead, I just got drunk on too-sweet cider and
gave your friend a massage
in front of you,
after you'd arrived and called me "sister."
I spat "brother" back at you.
This is how we went into our wounding.
Later, when you came over with your friends
for the fish you'd caught
(you needed a stove)
I asked you to stay–

obliviously. Drunkenly.
Desperately.
This was not the way I had wanted my plan
to unfold.
You were right when you told me that thing
that Freud said about attraction:
that repulsion lies in its shadow–
I couldn't stand you.
The previous night I had dreamed
that you had circled grammatical errors
on one of my essays–
even though I've studied this extensively and
reserve the right
to break the rules sometimes.
You are impossible.
You are always pulling away
when all I want is to ravage you
and spit you out.
You don't let me.
When talking about success with you that day:
the happy husband and wife Canadian Tire
            commercial–
you suggested that I didn't want it
because it felt off limits to me–
sour grapes.
I thought about it,
in a way that I doubt you'd consider
one of my reflections.
Since I suppose you think
you've already considered everything
in the universe
I guess
you figure that anything I say
is either well done
or misguided.
But what you gave me
two months ago,
your whole being present
in every movement and feeling,
the one you've so casually taken away from me
leaves me with a hunger
and a bitterness–

a door slammed in my face
and a lock I don't care to
break my skin trying to open anymore.
We are through.
And this is the last poem I'll ever write
about you.
This is how I go into my wounding.
This is how nothing is resolved.
This is how the hurt stays alive in me,
and festers its poison in my tissues.
A whole vine of grapes
sour now
from too much rain and
time spent on the branch,
wishing for things that will not come.

Hiding Places

His armor was so thick I couldn't get to
the place where he lived.
He hid behind his intellect, with
curtains drawn:
all I wanted to do was look inside–
I couldn't get through to his heart,
shattered,
his feelings of failure
and the son and daughter
he felt he let down.
I couldn't understand,
not having kids of my own,
and even when I tried,
he wouldn't let me.
His heartbreak was so thick
it blackened the air around us,
filled my nose with the stench
of a hundred rotting corpses.
I went to meet him at the dock,
the place where we met,
but he was somewhere on the other side
with a woman.
I left a message on his phone,
and marched away with water bottles
in both fists, resisting
looking back
at the sound of vehicles approaching.
I still had hope.
For some very lonely reason
I still had hope that he'd come and find me.

Sharp Things

I'm sitting inside your old heart
bathed in your scent, your soul
in milk crates–and all of those books
tell your stories: all of the things about you
I never found out.
All of ways in which I didn't
dig deep enough.
I believe
we could have gone further, had you just given me
a shovel, I could have dug
a grave for my jealousy,
placed it down there with my insecurities,
and my addiction to needing to know
all of your secrets–I could have
buried it with my cutting remarks and
hurt places where your hands never went.
I could have hidden it from view and even
earshot, the screaming of my trust
betrayed.
I could have disposed of it.
I believe
we could have made it work, had you just given me
a scalpel: I could have
cut into you and removed it–
that thing you couldn't stop doing; I could have
put it in the grave with my own addictions;
they could have found each other there
and fought it out for eternity, while we
got to know each other in newer and fuller ways.
Or maybe, with a little help they could have even
learned to love each other.
I think they needed us for that, though.
And we didn't have objects sharp enough
to deal with them.
I would have loved
to know your stories, your awkwardness,
your neurotic thoughts, and all of the ways
you second-guessed yourself.

I could have loved it all: your bursts of anger
and apologies, your struggles with loving
        yourself,
your convictions of your own inferiority.
I could have loved you through it all,
gone deeper into your well of self-pity.
I could have held you there until you found
a way out.
I believe we could have been happy, but all you
        gave me
were your tears, and the only sharp thing I
        could
find was a pencil. So I wrote poems
in your heart, and I posted them on the walls,
but you didn't live there any longer.

With A Hunger
I Didn't Know I Had

I will not Sell my Days for Gold

They deem me mad because I will not sell my days
for gold; and I deem them mad because they think
my days have a price.
-Khalil Gibran

I will not be around for another sunrise,
for another muffled morning in your sleepy house,
　　　your
cinnamon buns and Earl Grey, bathed in a seven
　　　o'clock glow,
your cantaloupe and polka dots, with all that
　　　breath
wafting out French doors. I will not
be there for your hardwood floors, your
forest walks and outdoor
showers, your towels of the plushest whites and
　　　greens, and
the pearls in your silken hair, neatly tied
into a knot, a bed
for a sacrificial crown made of blood.
Do not speak to me of dead prophets, books
of the dustiest
thickness, tombstones,
and all of those heavy blankets and cushions
you have
in your coffin for bones and rosaries.
Instead, find me in the aisles between
churches and brothels, communing with beggars
　　　and whores–
find me in downtrodden alleyways, scrawling
　　　transient verse
on cement and stone, my signature
to be whitewashed by men in blue coats who know
very little about what it means to be a breathing
　　　soul
with a pulse and a purpose and the understanding
　　　that
decades slide by like traffic on slick streets, and
　　　that

if you don't make your own reckless rhythms, if
        you don't
sleep in your tap shoes, or run barefoot, if
you keep tracing well-defined lines, you won't
know what it means to be living in this corner
        of the galaxy
at this time.
I will not be around to connect the dots,
everything you've worked for, will not be there
to inherit
your plasticine jewelry or gold-studded
        gramophones because
art is worth the struggle, and because I'd rather
spin like a drunken top in the rain than
watch all the fun from my wicker bench on the
        veranda,
knitting arthritic speculations about how it
        must feel
to be one so crazy, so broken, so foolish, and so
        free.

Will the Moon Ever be Full Enough?

Will she ever reach full term,
pregnant with the weight of her own company,
    her waist
fifty thousand light-years
in circumference, a sphere with a fortune
inside her. You shake her up
to see the snow fall, a blizzard: Montreal in
    December,
and what did it mean
to leave her family?
Will the moon ever be full enough? Twelve
    thousand bassinets and
baby doll dresses
for stillborn stars that died centuries ago; her
    mother
on the telephone now, and how
long distance calls used to cost
ten cents per minute, and back then that
was a lot.
Will her cup ever be full enough? Seven children
    and
a husband, and an embroidered tablecloth she
    began
as a maiden and finished as a widow–what time
elapsed in the in-between place? What sun
did she miss, when she was so busy
trying to paint the moon
on an oversized canvas–it didn't matter how
    much space
she had, it was never going to be enough; it sank
into the black hole she carried inside her, the
    way
black paint always swallows the white.
But she never painted with flames, moonbeams,
    or her own reflection, and maybe
had she tried
she would have found
that the light had the same effect
on the darkness.

Parasite

It's the way that lovers inevitably
change things–
meaningless objects with
next to no memory attached:
your Corn Flakes box and dirty yellow
foot pump–
I brought them back to you
with a note,
apologizing.
You didn't say a word–
you could barely look at me.
You still won't.
I walked home alone in the dark.
The blackberries in my front yard,
shrivelling now, by the road,
how confident and ripe they once were–
I used to pick them while you
threw disks in the field.
The woodpecker upon the post now,
in the mornings.
It is almost as if he is laughing at me.
You used to say he was laughing at me.
These things remind me now
of a man
whose heart was barred off to me;
whose soul was somewhere other than here.
And you are making me pay now
with your silence:
the only thing you have–
an absence of words and tears,
and I am wanting,
with a hunger I didn't even know
I had–with a longing
to be seen, and felt, and met
in the place where
we hurt each other.
All I receive is your rage,
seeping out your pores, a sweaty grudge,
permeating the air between us.

You are wounded.
I want to say,
Shout at me.
Tell me how angry you are.
Show me your heart,
ripped open–
I want to smell the blood.
I want to see all the ways in which you feel
I tore you apart.
But you won't grant me
the satisfaction
of knowing
that I meant something to you–
that maybe I was able to hurt you
because I found a wormhole:
I infested you,
the way that parasites always steal,
and replace their harvest with their eggs
and feces.
I would be flattered
if you'd grant me this title:
someone who had the power
to disturb the balance
in your heart.

Vigil

For three nights I paid observances
at the cathedral on Rue Longueil:
this was the second fire
your body had been through.
I suppose all your sins got burned away.
Candles lit up the inside.
The only light in that enormous darkness–
smell of hot wax and birthday cake for the dead,
and your picture stood by the wooden urn
with the cross on it–
the only thing that would survive another fire.
And next to your photograph were roses,
blazing hearts torn to threads,
bleeding into lacquered wood and
golden crosses, red,
crowns made of thorns
for a savior who needed saving.

Tonsillitis

I wake up alone on my couch–
the first time in weeks–with
tonsillitis:
the consequence
of too many lovers
and no love.
My throat on fire, it hurts
to swallow:
all of those words in my neck.
All of the things I dared not say.
I wanted to tell him
I used him too.
I wanted to tell him it's true,
what I said that morning at five o'clock
was crazy,
and I'm not sure why I even said it.
I wanted to fill the gap,
the void in my heart
the place
where you used to live,
and I suppose
still do.
And I was pulling on him,
his sleeve
almost completely off now, his shirt
twisted:
I was begging him
for the things I could not ask for.
I was begging him to give me the things
I wasn't willing to give back.
I wanted to mean something, be
something–own
something within him.
I wanted to create worlds with him:
a private place with a code
only the two of us had access to.
But wanting that was selfish, and I
was selfish for wanting it–
when he was just a distraction,

a bottle of wine,
a too-warm body in my bed and a pair of lips,
pulling air out of him.
Pulling dust: the remains
of a storage room
where his ex still lived.
And we were mirror images;
his wailing echoed my own
in the gorge
where our hearts used to beat.
How could I expect anything else?
He was damaged.
I suppose I was too.
She told me I need to get out of this pattern:
that I need
to enter relationships as myself; not
as the hurt little girl
who wants her father's love.
But the two are entwined, and I don't know
where she ends and where
I begin, or how
to distinguish myself from my pigtails,
my sidewalk chalk, my skipping rope,
my lollipops and dolls,
and all of those jelly bracelets.
I ride bicycles in loitered alleyways,
my banana seat still smudged
with my father's fingerprints,
the place
where he held on and eventually
let go.
And I am trying to navigate
on this road,
sometimes gravel, sometimes asphalt,
sometimes roaring with traffic,
wobbling and falling, and wanting
the memory of you.
I can't do this.
I'm terrified.
I can't find the balance.
I thought I knew who I was.
And when I'm not out of my mind

or in the arms
of another man, alone on my couch with
tonsils ripping, I am lost
and liquid
and taking the shape of the room.
I am vapor.
I am smoking my brains out and wafting out
open doors,
dissipating.

Gravity

I needed him like fire; like the sun; like the very thing I orbited around; he was my source of warmth; my energy; my light. And I loved him more than I loved myself, watery planet that I was: heavy with earth and emotion.

All of those nights I spent hugging my pillow against my heart, sinking, alone in that single bed at my sister's, back east, with feet hanging and blankets twisting, the stuffing that always gravitated to one end of the duvet cover. I was too lazy to rearrange it, or else too sleepy, or else too careless. I melted into that bed, with silence stapling its hooks into my spine, the long night stretching out like a blade, invisible under a moonless sky–and I was a book, with his words still written all over my skin. I had to slice off his syntax, layer by layer–even his silences had to go.

I didn't see the moon for months–my period my only reminder of her existence–that she came back in different shapes and sizes every night, that maybe she understood me. The ceilings were low. My window was small. I was usually asleep by ten.

Staying up late wasn't worth it anymore; for the first week Olivia fed me red wine and positive reinforcement until midnight, and I would flop into bed, too sedated to even text him.

But as the weeks wore on, reality set in like the coming of spring, thawed out the blanket under which I tried to hide–and my tears, like icicles, turned hot. I made a habit of holding myself, the way that he once did–my own arms around my body–talking to myself about things only I knew were true. It was the sanest thing I had done in months, with rain pouring on my roof–my igloo caving in. This is how I learned prayer: not on my knees with my hands clasped, or upturned to the sky, smiling, chanting the names of the lord, in Lotus–but curled up in a ball in a lumpy bed up north, clutching my ribs, sobbing, "I need help," imploring.

For weeks I'd begged him, in my most undignified robes, my knees scabbed black and red: a game of checkers I was destined to lose. I couldn't seem to get through a single telephone call without going back to it: an anchor; a magnet; a negative charge for my positivity of the notion that I couldn't survive without him, that it was all my fault–if it was, I figured we'd have a chance. Everything that he was and that I'd imagined.

On the morning that my heart slowed to fifty beats per minute, I barely minded or felt scared. I suppose it's difficult to feel scared when your heart is already barely beating–the same way it is to feel terrified when it's racing; a feedback loop. Still, I had a moment when, lying on cold linoleum, I thought of my life without him and wondered if it was worth it, the way the moon might feel without the sun's rays, illuminating. The way a tree must feel without earth, holding it still, nourishing.

And in ways I was a rootless tree, a hermit crab without a shell, the dark side of the moon–a vagabond who went from house to house, searching for a home, the lunatic on the grass living off borrowed air and stolen soil.

Old Enough to Believe in Magic

Neighbours

From two in the morning until two
in the afternoon I could hear them:
the crazy creaking bed, her moans, even his,
occasionally–
it sounded like he was going to kill her
with how much speed and force
he was putting into it.
They must be on Viagra, I laughed–
either that or cocaine.
No one fucks for this long,
and this hard
without help.
But secretly I was jealous
that two people so passionate,
who never give each other the silent treatment,
the way we do,
would rather claw or duke or scream it out
than keep it inside–
than try to punish the other
with a quiet so deafening
it hurts just to be in earshot.
It is true:
they should probably not
have kids, or live
anywhere near other people–
but what does it matter?
They are living their lives,
aren't they?
They are exploring what it means to love
and hate someone, in spurts or
all at once–
what it means to be
in a relationship.
Maybe they are living their lives
more fully than we are–
because they're not afraid to feel
the full range of emotions
that comes with being young, and crazy,
and in love, and not caring

what anyone else thinks of them.
Whenever you shout, I try to quiet you.
The neighbours will hear, I tell myself,
like my mother, so long ago now,
in her petal pink kitchen straight out of the 90's–
what will the neighbours say?
What happens in this house stays in this house.
But it always seeped out, somehow–
like cigarette smoke or room spray;
try to contain or disguise it all you want;
it will go wherever there is an open crack.
And I wonder what our neighbours think of us:
quiet, except for your music–
our voices and impressions,
which we deem funny–
the occasional whimper of pleasure or pain,
and the odd screaming or crying fit, mostly
from you, though I wonder,
am I really as discrete as I think I am?
I wonder what picture we paint of ourselves,
by the sounds that escape our flimsy door,
like incense.

Analog Quiet

You spend cold days
reading poetry by Christmas lights,
white, at four in the afternoon,
by real writers and their poetics,
conversations and interviews, on paper:
learning what Levertov said
about organic form, Atwood's poignant
      remarks
on contemporary scholarly attempts
at poetry dissection and what it means
to write well; how Plath couldn't live
without it–
you research Stevens,
Yeats, Pound–
books left in boxes and on shelves
since your undergrad, and you wonder
why you waited so long
to call upon them, this time
by choice.
And you prefer to write
on white paper now, gulping words and
honeyed tea,
looking things up in books, making
occasional calls home, but
from outdoor payphones, having cancelled
your monthly plan.
The world's gone
digital, you said–
even cigarettes
are electronic now.
Maybe the government is keeping tabs
on every puff–
counting down the dollars it'll save
on you
in forty years from now.
And you are as anonymous and independent,
in this second-floor apartment,
tucked away amongst the shops and cafes,
in this city of six hundred thousand,

classic and dependable, secretive and
        unassuming,
the way gramophones and top hats in attics
must feel.

Where are all the Juliets?

I am tired of this bourgeoisie and the word we
    use
to describe it, this
daily life, this predictable conversation
about how my day was, over a six-ounce glass
of Jackson Triggs–
I am so sick
of this town,
with its street kids and businessmen, the gap
into which I fall,
like a stone thrown
between cedar planks, with
salmon grilling, its juices sweetening
the breath between us.
I feel better
in my slippers and baggy jeans, reading
the local newspaper aloud, the
"I saw you" column–a tall guy with a beard and
    glasses
who saw a petite Asian woman
with a yoga mat at the bus stop on Commercial
    and Broadway:
he stepped on her Toms; she smiled at him;
he wants to go out for coffee.
And I am tired of this pretentiousness, this
Vancouver-ness,
the classic cafe suggestion.
Why not ask her to carve Jack-O-lanterns in
    January,
or walk on rooftops, or
take a bus out of town and see what happens?
I suppose no one wants to take chances
    anymore.
But I want to know where the romantics are
    these days, and why
the "I Saw You" section, straight out of the 90's,
seems to be reserved for men with beards and
    skinny women
in Hunter boots.

Every once in a while you hear
that an eighteen-year-old girl with blue hair
and a half-sleeve saw a thirty-two-year-old
      woman at a rave.
She was on MDMA for the first time, and she
      wants to make out again.
But that isn't that romantic, either.

People called us by our last names

I met him at the A frame
in the North end
in the woods
the place
where my friend was squatting with
no electricity or running water
a paradise
for hippies
tea lights and tequila
he drank at ten in the morning
because it was there
he drummed on anything with a surface
even my hips
he said those were his favourite
and the ease
with which we greeted one another
together on that recliner
tipping backwards and how
I wasn't even shy
about dancing or singing or speaking
in accents or picking
his nose
we were farting within hours
and we lazed around in the late-afternoon
talking about nothing in particular
there were so many questions
I could have asked but somehow
I didn't have to
in a past life
we were a married Indian couple
Rajesh and Sunita
we picked up where we left off
with conversations flowing
he read by flashlight
while I slept
I cut his hair on a sunny morning
and drank his coffee
an accident
he said he didn't care that

the cup wasn't washed
and told me I ought to quit
showering because
he wanted to smell my pheromones
and he was a washboard playing gypsy
a single dread lock
adorning his head
the kind of man I felt
would get bored with me
straight-laced
as I was sure I was
I threw
moss all over my face and breasts
the point where sexy becomes
weird
he brought it out in me
this kookiness
amplified
I loved that...
who I was around him

Where the Burdock Grows

She told me she used it for cleansing–
that it was great for the liver and skin,
said she'd never felt so grounded in her life;
and she harvested the roots like magic limbs,
put them into her wicker basket.
For tinctures, she said.
For tea.
For later when she
throws them into her secret garden
and goes to the land of giants.
And I still don't understand nude beaches,
still feel uncomfortable
around those who run wild
amongst nettles under crescent moons
in Scorpio, still
don't know how to dance
at afternoon markets, or anywhere
without at least a bit of booze.
I still can't sleep in my new room,
uncertain as I am:
terrified as I am–
unused to it as I am:
sleeping without you.
We sit at the ocean's edge talking
about her great loves–
men with Native names and men who taught her
all about the healing secrets of mushrooms,
men who held her while she sobbed–
even the woman she dated who brought her to
        the hospital
when she accidentally snorted Heroin.
She is open to love again.
She wants to move to the mountains:
somewhere more rugged,
where rivers flow.
And I just arrived on this island, soft
with saltwater and rolling slopes,
all my beans in her basket–
my shattered heart bleeding all over my clothes.

And I don't know how to harvest Burdock,
or what it does,
and I don't really care.
I am exhausted,
homeless,
and lost
in a forest of plant medicine
with many pharmaceutical interactions.

Penny Fountain

It was one of those fountains–
you know,
the kind in malls, where teenagers loiter,
in ripped jeans,
tongue kissing each other and cussing,
chewing gum.
But this fountain was green and quiet, with
tiny tiles
squiggly
from the water,
like a pool,
with no life in it–
except for the fairies,
which sang beautiful haunting songs,
but no one else could hear them.
And my mother used to give me pennies
to throw in it.
I held them in my chubby little girl hands,
closed my eyes, and
wished
for my grandpa to come back to life,
knowing that he probably wouldn't,
but I was still young enough to believe in magic.
This was one year after the cancer got into his bones,
and he passed away in a coma,
though I heard
in recent years
that even in those last hours
he suffered and struggled
quite a bit.
I wonder if he entered a new body then,
if I'd recognize his eyes,
grey as smoke,
and as translucent,
looking lovingly at me,
from the cradle, from my arms–
would I know it
if he came back?
And I wonder if all he was waiting for

from his ethereal blue sky,
was a little girl to wish upon a dirty mall fountain
for his return.
If the fairies heard me,
they never did confirm.
But I believe that he's in the world
somewhere now–
because I'm old enough to believe in magic again,
though I try not to throw money away now.

Waiting for Take-Out

I sit
at the Indian buffet place,
on a bench,
waiting for my take-out:
two pieces of naan to go
with our homemade paneer,
when I see you
across the room,
against the rainy
windowpane.
You look sad.
Bored.
Fucking depressed,
if you want to know the truth,
sitting there before a full dish,
with a man
stuffing his face,
and a little girl,
eating from both your plates, not
touching her own.
I wonder if she thinks this is normal.
And I wonder what happened
to cause
you such sadness; what happened
to the little girl you used to be,
exploring different spices from
giant plates
that weren't set in front of you,
and that you therefore weren't
forced to swallow.

Anything But Hallelujah

Klin

Raincloud canopy,
the colour of the moon–
nothing really changes here.
And I'd like to send a crater
through the haze, poke a hole
in the boredom, or at least
come home for Christmas.
I'd like to be in your little house
beside the frozen lake, all of us
warm in sweaters next to the wood stove,
thawing,
talking freely; candidly; at times even impolitely,
or else up in my room with the giant window
     and
some of my artwork still on the walls,
while you watch TV, and I
lament the loss of human connection in my
     journal,
or else take hot baths in your big tub and
wrap myself in your fluffy towels,
white as snow,
that don't smell of mold or only cover
half of my body.
And I remember snow, like anyone else from the
     north–
the perpetual storm of 2006, looking outside,
from the laundry room in the basement,
in that dingy apartment building
on Bruce Street, sitting there washing and
watching my clothes,
reading snippets of The Republic for homework;
the first snow when I was just five years old,
and Jenn woke me up, saying, "There's snow in
     the cupboards!"
looking for Mapo-spread and butter speckled
with toast crumbs
before finding my red mittens and going out to
     play;
the time you built a cabin with me,

but on our patio, closed for the season,
dragging the toe of your boot across the snow,
making lines,
the way we'd make houses in schoolyard gravel.
And I remember snow in my back,
hot tears streaming down frozen cheeks,
skiing with dad,
telling me how I could improve,
devastated that I wasn't making him proud,
        trying
to hide the lump in my throat, the heat in my
        sinking heart.
I remember the snow all over the neighbourhood
        kids'
faces and coats, the screams and laughter
from beyond the window pane.
"Why don't you go and join them?" you said.
But I was shy.
And the feeling returned nearly twenty years
        later,
alone in an orchard after the first snow—
him having snowball fights with her and the rest,
and I, too timid, or too weak, or too resentful
to join.
I sat in the field, snow soaking my seat,
hearing your voice: "Why don't you join them?"
It's just not who I am, I guess.
It's just not how I'm made.
The snows separate the years for me:
mark them with white lines carved on closed
        patios,
dividing time like rooms.
Of course, we were both a lot younger then.

October

You wanted to know what October tasted like. You wanted to see it, orange and golden, burst open like a sunset between your lips, like acorns, like chrysanthemums, like quail eggs, like quince.

You said you wanted to smell it: a wood stove with cedar smoking–in your stomach: early evening upon earlier evening, still, stretching out: a garden upturned and mulched, the rot of compost, the coming cold, a sea of Sundays, the blood moon you swear you won't miss, but you do.

You said you wanted to hear it: dry leaves crunching under brown boots, twigs snapping in the late afternoon, the weight of walking through maple forests, crimson, with your father, his feet popping pebbles and sticks, poplar and pine, and wind whirling, raindrops pregnant as tears hitting your forehead and your eyes wetting your cheeks.

But most of all you wanted to feel it: the void in your chest, the sky gunmetal, the end of summer, and all that grass gone to seed, with reeds brown and beige, the boredom, the dock vacant, all of your friends somewhere other than here, except for you and the clam shells. It is almost as if during the night or when no one was watching someone or something submerged it, or as if the pond regurgitated its contents–a stomach sick from too much tequila and beer.

What happens after everyone has gone home for the season, to light fires and curl up with sweaters and sweethearts? You sling your pack over your shoulders. You soldier south in the rain: a sole goose searching for warmth, her flock somewhere else, the missing piece of a faraway V, with headlights and more headlights flying by. Speedily, with songs of summer still serenading you–songs you're not yet willing to give up–you float in your own river, waters still warm and deceiving.

Your hat, brown as roots, your sleeves pulled down, your knees still scabbed grey as soot, and all the things you promised to release, swirling, as you wonder if you'll succeed this time.

With October you're given another chance: to sink into your bones, as if into a steaming bath, with cold sodden leaves falling on your knees and forearms, your pores opening like eyes, seeing how well you accept death–the changing of weather–how well you slide into acceptance of the rainy day, the coming of night, and how you embrace the lessons Scorpio has been trying to teach you since you were first imagined into inception: this bittersweet cycle of birth, sex, and death–a violin solo that is bound to leave you weeping, and one that is always done too soon.

Brain Buddy

We were both sick when we met;
our therapist hooked us up.
I guess she thought it'd be good for us–
you know...
to have someone to talk to.
We met in the boardroom that August: my hair
    down
and my curve-hugging pants on, and I realized
I should have taken an Ativan, and you
asked me what I was thinking about
when my eyes welled up.
"My eyes aren't welling up."
We shared our stories: the drugs, the sedation,
the hospitalizations: delusions and
    hallucinations–
how you thought you stopped the war in Syria
    with your mind,
and I was convinced
my parents were evil spirits–
things you don't tell people you've just met–
but these were special circumstances, and I
    figured that
made it alright.
The next thing I know it's November, and we're
sitting a hole-in-the-wall pub, after beer and
deep-fried pickles, making attempts at covering
    the
silence settling in,
like a blanket of snow,
and you take a deep breath and almost shout,
Want to go to the Festival of Lights?
I'm pleased that you don't want the evening to
    end.
I'm pleased that you like my company.
Next, we're both
more than a little drunk, making out in my
    sister's
empty hot tub in the basement.
Maybe we wanted to feel normal again.

I think we both wanted to feel normal again.
The story ends in early December,
after a few silent meals at dimly lit restaurants
where you pick up the bill,
and I feel bad,
knowing your only income is your Disability
      pension–
like me.
I say nothing.
For now, we're just two adults having dinner
      together.
For now, it's like nothing happened to render
      us
nearly incapable of conversing, or listening
without wondering which eye to look into
or when to blink or stir.
I tell you now that no, I don't want to have
      dinner again
on Monday evening.
I tell you I don't feel much of a connection
      between us.
You respond with, Sometimes life hands you
      little surprises.
You say that I was one of them.
And so we go back to our quiet lives
in our respective towns,
as if you didn't spend two days in my basement
      bedroom,
drinking Cracked Canoe and staring at
      Christmas tree lights,
talking nonsense about anything, pausing to
      fuck or nap
with your arm around my body,
or like you didn't drive me to my housekeeping
      job at seven a.m.,
sending me off with a bagel and a Tim Horton's
      coffee
and a smile on my lips.
The whole thing was too good to be true–
two people with the same condition
who understood what it meant to be
      marginalized,

stigmatized, penalized for the mechanics of
    their minds,
making a go at the dating scene,
which is taken away from so many people
turned mental patients,
with nothing to offer a world so cold and
    confused,
with such a limited understanding of what it
    means to be worth loving.

Good Friday

It always rains: the sky
a chalky slate,
with no poetry written on it:
nails scratch,
get hammered into open palms
that once healed a hundred lepers.
This is not a day for tulips and daffodils.
Your black coat, a shroud,
a cover for crosses and holy water:
hood your head,
look down at your feet, inching forward;
your lips sewn shut,
abstaining from chocolate and chatter.
Hymns, sober as silence, and as somber,
sing of anything
but Hallelujah.
Do not deny your part in this now,
like Peter and the rest of the Jews,
who knew not what they did,
because you do–
and you've been doing it all your life:
remember the daily crucifixion
of the Christ
you carry with you:
the kingdom of God is within–
and if you are not the very incarnation
of Jesus:
the son or daughter of the Divine, tell me,
who are you?

Glass Blower

I was drunk when I first
met you–half a bottle of wine
and my unoriginal flirt coming out:
I braided your hair and guessed
your sun sign.
Later, I couldn't remember your first name,
but had the distinct recollection
that you were a Virgo.
You told me, months later,
that you were afraid that people
would think you were boring.
And I loved your confessions,
your realness,
the dirt beneath your nails,
the smell of a working man,
and all that glass blown
into poetry:
self-deprecation and all the things
you shouted
when you weren't saying a thing.
How you held me when I told you
how nervous I was
about reading my poems in crowded rooms.
My vulnerability didn't scare you.
And I loved your oversized tee shirts,
your jeans that didn't
show off your body–
the fact
that you hadn't had your picture
taken in years, and how
you claimed to not be photogenic.
And in ways we were opposites–
all of the things I disliked
about myself, a perfect
contradiction:
my face in mirrors, and the knowledge
of which angles worked for me–
your naked belly you said
you didn't like; you were beautiful

in your self-consciousness, in
your sincerity, in
your modesty, in
your unawareness of your own
naturalness, in your
quietness.
It is true; I have a weakness
for blue eyes and
understatement–men who
seem to have no clue
of their own gentleness,
their own warmth,
their own protectiveness–
their own strength
that does not require
flashing lights or
florescent colours.
And I wonder
if my fascination with you
holds up a mirror
to all of the things I do not see
myself being–
the scents and lines and sounds,
the music I exude,
blind and deaf and paralyzed
and unaware
of the things I also shout
in the silences, in the dark,
in the secret places where
the heart
is the only witness.

Coyote

Whenever loneliness comes back,
like weeds and other perennials, reveals
her yellow petals
from inside my chest, I feel her–
she is unmistakeable–
the smell of rain on cement–
and I recognize her like an old friend
poking through sidewalks:
chalk dust and worn out denim;
stale coffee and gasoline;
empty corridors and a sad harmonica–loyally
awaiting my return:
in hot baths
up to my chin; in my car
winding down cold and familiar roads
at dusk;
in steaming cups of tea; in heartbreak; in
Sunday afternoons; in music
from long ago: the silence after the party.
Sounding a lot like my voice cracking
the dark in two,
telling me things only I know are true;
soaking my pillow with tears.
I recognize loneliness so well
I even saw her in you:
floating across the country
like dandelion fuzz
on a breeze blowing in from the west: old dreams
enveloping me
in nostalgia and
quiet, melancholy music–the bare wires and raw
nerve endings, the realness
of your words, secrets I recognized as my own:
our separate stories lived together, somehow.
It was as if we had always been lovers.
Sometimes I wonder if it's you that I miss,
or if it's just a companion for my aloneness–
your coyote hymn that said,
I'm with you in this seclusion:

two song dogs exchanging glances
on a diverging path
overgrown with yellow flowers.

My Words in a Heart-Shaped Locket

Farmers' Market at nine a.m.

Don't you love
the smell of wood smoke and
early-morning markets?
October and the promise
of bicycles with baskets and beetroot
at the shop up the street,
where old men in turbans playfully banter
with customers in an attempt to sell a single
talisman or stick of sandalwood.
Is there anything in this sold out world
quite like a yoga class at sunrise–
sweat and breath
in a wooden room with high ceilings and
brick walls–
inspiration, autumn apples,
bright mittens, travel mugs, and
running up sidewalks shouting,
"This is the best day of my life!"
with your glowing face
rising with the sun, shouting:
"And I'm not even usually up by now!"
Was there ever anything quite so lovely
as pinwheels, warm and gooey,
sold by wholesome vendors,
leg warmers in every colour,
and nothing to do all day but write?
Seven years later I wonder,
was there ever anything
so deliciously lonesome
as remembering a best friend,
a hometown,
spontaneous outings, and
days thought uneventful, spent
biting into fall
with all of our youth,
our freedom,
our ideals
rising on the strings of some mandolin
on Elm street, case open, hoping for change:

with the future still illusive as the air in our lungs,
as close,
and as sweet.

Woodsman

He was the kind of man who belonged
in the woods, who got better
with every passing heartbeat, every ring
in his trunk, every forest fire. His temper
cooled with
the passing of his father, and then
his mother, his rebellious
teenage girls who
smoked crack,
or else refused to eat,
or else studied English Literature
rather than Science,
his blood pressure elevating
from a lifetime of greasy food
and anger fueled by what he could not control.
He was the kind of man
who had softened, let
the years wear off his bark,
an Arbutus;
he became
a sweet and solid voice, a Maple,
at the end of the telephone line, the branch
that tied me to him, and his heart
was the same colour as mine,
and it didn't matter anymore that
we spent our lives disagreeing because
when he wasn't looking I became
a willow, and he, in response,
did too.

Plow

The city beams
through your blinds,
like a too-bright smile,
on the second floor:
plastering on the charm
like a Monroe poster, her dress
every bit as white,
and as phony
as her teeth,
sharp as the claws
between her thighs.
The garbage truck flashes past
like the plow on bright white nights
in Northern Ontario, post snowstorm,
when everything sounds muffled now, safe, now–
and the streets are almost warm.
And you are exhilarated, fresh
from an attic jam session
by an open window
at a house in Japan, while I
write about my depression
in books not meant for reading.

Salt Spring Island

I drink in this scene like poetry, like peonies,
like a kiss from a lover absent for many seasons.
The park in this July morning, harbour in the
east, sun shining on still waters, shimmering,
boats anchored there: like magnets. Like
boulders. Like bullfrogs upon lily pads–si-
lent–eating bugs.

Men adjusting their pants at the waist, and
women in carefully chosen rags with guitars
slung around their bodies–like arrows. Like
swords. Women in last night's clothes with
takeout coffee from the roasting company
down the street. Queens. Men flashing their
art at me–like smiles and guns and hundred-
dollar bills. The currency around here is not
one of diamonds. People want soul here. They
want talent. Something with a pulse. They
want heart. Originality. Someone who under-
stands; someone with a gentleness. Men who
think they're going to woo all these women
with their artfulness, their skillfulness, their
love of language and texture, rhythm and col-
our. But my relationship with sound and si-
lence is a private one, and I'm not interested in
your take on things, your interpretations, your
feedback, or your opinions or critiques of what
channels through my heart and hands. I drink
the words in like sandalwood, like rose oil, like
homemade zucchini relish in October after-
noons–my mother's kitchen window open, and
my father's burn pile smoking. My red toque,
and the smell of Sunday– I drink the loneliness
like a slow song, a steaming bath, a brine:
green tea shared amongst women in a summer
kitchen in the mountains– our laughter echo-
ing and multiplying– there were five of us, no
seven, no ten. Thirteen women making black-
berry jam, and the supervisor in a meeting.
Actually, there were only two of us. Aprons and

kerchiefs–ladies of the past–taking part in this ancient ritual of preserving tradition. Rubber boots and plaid shirts.

When I made the front page of the monthly newsletter in my navy blue sweater, holding plump yellow peaches, their fuzzy skin bursting, heavy with sunlight, he said it felt invasive to read the article–like he was intruding into my life. I didn't have the same qualms; I read his journal. I drank his shame and his secrets like ink, like velvet, like midnight. They were delicious, like black magic and bruised flesh: his relationship with sound and silence. Voodoo.

When I finally told him the truth he went for a long walk around the golf course and asked for signs. Came back calm as a cucumber and told me we couldn't do this anymore. The gods had spoken, and there was nothing either of us could do to save the relationship. The colour blue. He drank it in: like sky; like rain; like the second full moon of the month of March. Like ice and fire. When things get cold or hot enough they always turn blue. A drowning man. A lotus flower. A pair of floating shoes that never quite find the dance floor.

Heart Geography

I spent two years in your shell
a sea turtle with nowhere else to go
nowhere else I wanted to go
even when I thought I wanted to leave
my heart was where you were
moving in and out
with the moon
with the tides
with you
and all of those glowing fish
points of light
more stars than sea
swimming
making me dizzy
I wished for solid ground
for a place where an imminent tsunami
didn't threaten to swallow me whole
for home
as I called it
where my family and friends lived
I thought they'd drop everything
I thought they'd make everything okay for
my heart torn
in two provinces at once
the more people I loved
the more places I wanted to be
How do I map
this geography
all of the places in which I have left
a piece of myself
all of our memories and big plans
Alex
your name burns in my chest
a flaming sword
stabbing and stealing
tears roll down my cheeks
I sob like a little girl
who has lost her childhood
I do not know where to go

what to do
how to go back to the place where I lost you
and put my heart back together
pick it up
a pile of mush
with shards of shattered seashells in it
and stuff it back inside my chest
take it with me
to a place where I feel
I can be myself
to a place where I will always
hold it close
a precious stone
a shell of my own
a home
in which I can rest
safe in my own love
and never let it get away again

Rose Quartz

Darling, you need to know that
Love created you:
how could you be or do
anything else?
And when you're jealous
and judging, know
that this is just
misinformed appreciation
for the other.
And when you're heartbroken,
know
that it's just your beating heart
you're feeling,
and you didn't know
that Love
was clearing the path
for even more love.
And when you're angry,
you need to know
that when you're coming
from your truth
anger is your best friend and
fiercest protector.
And you need to know
that Love is not always soft–
sometimes it cuts the heads off demons.
Sometimes it wears their skulls around
        its neck.
And baby,
you are the most beautiful one
of your kind, the only one
who smells and feels and dances
quite like you.
You'd better love yourself
even when you can't manage it–know
that you are always held,
and cared for,
and protected,
and there is nowhere to go

in this universe of love
that is not bathed in the glow
of the Light that you are.

Flawed Perfection

I love you in your honesty,
your courage
to say how you feel,
even when it isn't convenient,
even when it isn't popular–
love you in your insecurities,
your negative self-talk–
all of the things you hate about yourself:
I love them all.
How you feel stagnant most of the time,
unable to make a positive change,
and I love you in your rawness,
how hugging yourself and saying,
"I love you" brings you to tears.
I adore you in your loneliness,
your melancholy blue eyes
with so much sadness in them,
love you in your elation,
your impersonations,
the little things that make your heart
sing,
and your music:
my sole companion on those nomadic trails,
the melody capturing my words
into a heart-shaped locket.
I love you in your guilt,
your lies,
your fear of telling me the truth:
all of those moments in which you were not strong.
I love every inch of your body
you are convinced is too fat–
and I love your awkwardness
in social situations, how you never say
the right thing,
but it's always genuine and real and endearing,
and perfect
because it's you,
and I love you
exactly as you are:

in all of your perfection deemed flawed.
I even love your refusal
to want me back–
love you through my rejection, and how
you're still there for me,
crying on the phone together, still,
helping each other through the one thing
we think we can't
help each other through.
I love every part of you, every toe nail,
every cell, every terrifying thought.
I just wish I loved you enough to let you go.

A Safe Place

Drugs that Restrain

You wanted my blood, my moonlit soul
all silvery, slithering
out of my veins,
and you
putting in orders: a vial of black sludge. I
    suppose
you wanted it for your neck.
For your refrigerator. For your pile of wretched
    secrets
and fishing trips, seven hearts and how
although I'd been cut up, I went on living.
I couldn't thank you
for your concern.
And I was speaking
in tongues, trying to feel
the difference, trying to taste
the language, the texture of syllables
that escaped without proper planting or
    watering,
the absence of meaning. I choked
and gagged on
a handful of words. More dirt than was
prescribed by the doctors observing
my behaviour in
padded cells, my telephone screaming and no
    one
to answer it.
Cadavers littered the churchyard;
a handful of anti-psychotics
I gagged on,
I still don't think I really needed the medicine,
    but took it
to keep the voices at bay: a grail of maggots and
    worms.
I was already awaiting my burial, and you
were collecting my life force in a syringe
    plunged into my chest:
a priest siphoning wine from the cross–
I decayed beneath those church walls, drowning

in holy water, and you
gulping my insides like Ayahuasca,
I remembered the pills
I swallowed, and laughed because my blood was
     bound
to send you reeling:
a sobriety that maddens.

A Hundred Letters to the Sea

He wrote a hundred letters
to the sea–
threw them
off the ferry: letters
to his ex-wife
–Sam–
who will not give him the time of day,
the closure he needs.
Who will not give him
the respect, the honoring
of what has passed, who will not
provide
the comfort he craves,
the acknowledgment
of his heartbreak, or meet him there
with hers.
Who will not bathe him in her tears,
or let him know she still loves him.
Who will never read the letters,
or find him in the depths,
the secret broken place
where he lives,
and does not want to leave.
He still has hope she'll come meet him there.
Whenever we're together he talks about her,
the festering sores that will not heal–
he carried her with him for two years;
he did not want to erase her,
or cover up her scent
with the smell of another woman.
Even now, he still holds her close.
She is in the van with us,
in the back, where the mattress is,
in his heart,
spilling out his mouth:
all that he'd hoped and wished for;
all that he could not have.
The stories of burning their life up:
setting their old house on fire:

the madman in the back yard–
after she took off with both kids.
He was hoping she'd meet him
at the counsellor's,
a chance to heal the rift–
a chance
to finally say all the things
they did not say–
(he rewrote his letter four times)
but she picked up an extra shift
at work.
And he is left
with a void
filled with her ghost:
as cold,
and as elusive,
and provides me with a similar
feeling–
his heart
always somewhere other than here,
his eyes
looking off in the distance,
the split
getting larger between us, with
arguments setting in.
All that I'd hoped for and could not have.
So I write letters to the sea as well–
as one of the women he wouldn't let in–
as one of the women who was just not Sam.
As one of the many women
who will never have the power
to fill and eventually abandon
the haunted places in his heart.

Snowy Ties

For weeks after we split I walked the railway bed,
sodden, pregnant with water;
you could have wrung out the ties, long black
        sleeves
left outside overnight, or drenched with tears.
I still go out, with
snow on the tracks, and my
tracks in the snow;
the only ones to be found there.
I thought about what ties connected me with other
        places:
where you left me by a raging river
swallowing even your name
I shouted
until my voice went hoarse and quickly
disappeared, the way winds
swallow even the deepest footprints.
I had it in my head that you would track me down.
I made my way back up the hill in my bare feet.
I took the old logging road back to the highway and
        hitched
back south, and stayed
in a dingy motel room that night:
mossy rugs and splintered mirrors–
the kind of place with scratchy yellow blankets
where people get murdered.
It was still dark when I walked to the train station
        the next morning.
These tracks hold us together in my mind, and
        though
I do not know where you are, I walk
northward on these ties after snowfalls,
and in the muffled cold without even the sound
of a faraway train,
I think of you, and where you might be:
with your new family, somewhere.
As far away as you could get from me and the
        memory
of how I led you down a mountainside and brought

you
to a river, promising hot springs, but left you
        there
barefoot, without a car to get you back home.
And maybe a crime against a human heart is less
        forgivable
than one against bones and blood.
Hearts are less resilient, somehow.
They are less forgetful.
Still, I walk along railway beds on quiet January
        afternoons,
leaving tracks on tracks behind me,
like breadcrumbs chewed up and swallowed;
It's only the wind, the witch replied.
It is impossible to find my way back home.

Come Closer

In the midst of losing
everything: with Saturn
the only one
returning:
job, school, you,
even my memory went–
who had said what to whom?
What classes did I teach
this morning?
What did I eat for dinner?
A vague recollection
of a split
in my mind–
I slid
down a flight of stairs,
a knife
across my white throat.
A ribbon appeared, as silken
as the red sea, and as miraculous;
she tore it out of my hand–
five foot two and barely one hundred
pounds–her mother bear,
her dragon,
her adrenaline,
she was twelve feet tall now, and
strong as the monster I was convinced
she was,
but with a heart.
The stories that repeat,
the memory that is lost.
Is it the pills?
The doctor tells me to quit drinking.
I don't, though,
because I've lost you,
and I need
kisses and wine, and
summer days that fade and stretch and melt
into each other; a journey slithering
into itself, a snake:

hiss, hiss–with Adam gone and nothing to
comfort me now but scales and a god
who won't forgive me.
I fade in and out of gardens now,
feet in wet earth, with
carrots pulling and
cabbages ripping–
a good year for tomatoes, of course
it hasn't really rained in months,
save for the drizzle
we had in July
when everyone down the road was cheering.
Fucking hippies.
I guess I'm one of them because I cheered too,
and you know,
I was barefoot and wearing a
bamboo skirt.
Couples make me sick:
arms around each other, enjoying
every
minute.
I remember your silhouette dancing
around the pond
at night, the yellow lights on
in the library, and
photographs of all those sinewy poses.
Fresh Slice at six o'clock and
sober.
You were frugal,
I'll give you that.
But I don't know what to do now,
swaying in and out of days that rise
like waves
and swallow me,
release me into the sea,
raging bathwater–
I am seasick.
I am tired.
I am lost.
I am frightened,
and I don't
know how to get back home.

My father's face,
the way it looked in the eighties, before
his jaw went chubby and his mustache white,
I love you, Dad.
You don't accept me, he shouts.
I love you, I say,
stronger this time, treading, and floating,
and pitching and rolling.
In the water I know how to stand
in my power.
It must be the tide;
too much Cancer in my chart.
Earth man, can you love me anyway?
Can you love the one who only knows
the language of the moon?
We are different.
And I love that about us.
Of course, this kind of intimacy only happens
in dreams.

Little Things

Barefoot coffee-drinking
and early-morning bathrobes.
Time-taking and other delights.
How luxurious it is to spend
a cold sunrise wrapped in silence.
You read by lamplight in the other room.
We are well-fed and rested.
And now, to hit the cold shower,
preparing for the day's work.
"I will enjoy it," I say.
"I am grateful."
But really all I want to do is sit here and write,
and stretch the year out into a sea of mornings.
How beautiful it is to relish a
beginning like this one–
with so many possibilities.

You can't Bottle the Stars

Even though I prayed and chanted, cast spells
for peace and visualized, in vain, and
even though I put
my best intentions behind it,
the crucifixion of Christ was planned
for centuries before it happened;
and those with pull have
elected a murderer: a villain
to force his way into your most basic human rights,
poison your water and brand even your breath
with his name.
There is nothing
more terrifying than a puppet in power
who does not know the sound of his own heart,
who isn't acquainted with the Sacredness of life,
who spits on it with stolen saliva reeking of money
and ignorance.
I want to provide a safe place
for every woman,
every refugee,
every person who is not of the mind
that they can rape a Goddess
and live to brag about it–a place
to run for shelter, where life
hasn't been stolen and sold
at a price so cheap
that no one can afford.
My wish
is that you remember what's true,
what's right, and what's good in the world
because you're going to have
to fight for it.
If you are courageous, you might say the same
about yourself.

Fare Forward Voyagers

You slide the record, smooth and cool,
out of its jacket,
like a lover who has walked many snowy miles,
and carefully
let it fall out of the sleeve with the smell
of the seventies, the whole decade captured
between cardboard, a time capsule for the nose,
into an open palm,
and place it, delicately, on the record player.
You move the needle to the outer edge,
place it down,
and hear the crackling begin.
Then the guitar, crisp as autumn leaves,
or as a starched shirt not touched since the
        baby boomers
were born–so close;
it is almost as if he is in the room with you.
Someone has cared for this record,
sweetly; softly–
someone has been very deliberate and
        tenacious
about keeping it in its original condition.
I imagine the wall-unit or shelf it must have
        adorned
in London, halfway across the world–
in a flat thick with posh accents and expensive
furniture–
I imagine the record must have kept someone
        warm
during the rainy season, with its songs lighting
        up
the evening, next to the glowing fireplace.
Why did that person decide to sell such a lovely
        piece
of art–and one that was taken care of so well?
Did the owner die? Of pneumonia or
        tuberculosis,
or some other impossibly romantic condition?
Imagine it: drowning on land.

Conditions that have a much different reality.
Maybe his wife didn't see the point in keeping
        all his records,
just wanted to get rid of them while she still
        could–
maybe the sound reminded her of him too
        much.
Maybe it was too pervasive, the way a
        nostalgic smell
can dig its way into the tissues of your heart,
gnaw away at it like an apple, and leave it,
a core, until you become desensitized
to what it feels like to smell something
        so close,
so raw, and so real–until you've become used
        to it,
and it fails to catch you by the throat
        anymore,
or stick in your lungs.
And so you continue to listen to this album,
enjoying the warm sounds and
the familiar foreign scent;
when you take it out, it is an experience,
a trip back to a time you did not live through,
but that you recognize from your father's
        poetry anthologies
he stole from school–
because the words and rhythms were so
        intoxicating,
he smuggled them like Southern Comfort in
        his backpack
all the way home, into boxes, and into new
        homes,
the books gathering the dust of different
        places
with every move. The pieces warmed his
        blood
on nights that he found himself alone and in
strange places.
Eventually, he stopped reading Eliot and
        Hopkins–
he got married. He didn't feel the need

118

to be comforted by words any longer,
choosing rather the warm breast and bright
      wings
of his wife–and I wonder if that's what happened
      to the man
who owned this Fahey record.
He had kids. He got so caught up in long hours
      at the office,
rugby tournaments and parent-teacher
      interviews,
that he left his collection to collect dust.
Perhaps they learned to take care of themselves,
the way orphans inevitably do.
They remain on shelves, untouched,
their musk growing like moss or algae.
But now the record is yours–
in your tiny apartment in downtown Toronto,
as you attempt to make a living and pay back
your student loans–
as you wonder what kind of life you want to live–
as you wonder when you'll meet that sweet soul
who will love you for all of your dark and light
      parts,
the whole of you, lit up like a torch
in the rainy season.

Made in the USA
Charleston, SC
29 December 2016